Time and the seasons

The In My World Series

Bobbie Kalman
Susan Hughes

Toronto
New York Crabtree Publishing Company

The In My World Series
Created by Bobbie Kalman

Writer:
Susan Hughes

Editor-in-Chief:
Bobbie Kalman

Editors:
Rachel Atlas
Susan Hughes
Lise Gunby

Cover and title page design:
Oksana Ruczenczyn, Leslie Smart and Associates

Design and mechanicals:
Catherine Johnston
Nancy Cook

Illustrations:
Title page by Karen Harrison
Pages 28 and 30 by Deborah Drew-Brook-Cormack
© Crabtree Publishing Company 1985
Pages 4-31 and cover © Mitchell Beazley Publishers 1982

Cataloging in Publication Data

Kalman, Bobbie, 1947–
    Time and the seasons

(The In my world series)
ISBN 0-86505-072-4 (bound) –
ISBN 0-86505-094-5 (pbk.)

1. Time – Juvenile literature. 2. Seasons –
Juvenile literature. I. Hughes, Susan, 1960–
II. Title. III. Series.

QB209.5.K34   1986   j529′.7

To Carly

350 Fifth Avenue
Suite 3308
New York, N.Y. 10118

102 Torbrick Road
Toronto, Ontario
Canada M4J 4Z5

Contents

What time is it?

Time is hours and seconds, mornings and nights. It is days, weeks, months, and years. We can see time through the things that change around us. Day becomes night. Spring becomes summer. The past becomes the present, and the present will soon be the future. Time is always with us. Let's learn more about time!

Telling time

Ken and his father have just bought new watches. Watches and clocks are instruments that measure time. Ken's father is teaching Ken how to tell time. He explains that each day is divided into twenty-four hours. Most clocks and watches count to twelve twice each day. Each hour is divided into sixty minutes. On watches like the one Ken's father is wearing, there is a short hour hand and a long minute hand. The hour hand points to the number of the hour. The minute hand counts the minutes that make up each hour.

Ken's watch is a *digital* watch. It does not have hands. It has numbers that change as the time changes. When it is noon, the watch reads 12:00. An hour later, the watch reads 13:00 or one o'clock in the afternoon. Two hours later, the watch reads 15:00. What is another way Ken could say 15:00?

Picture talk

Which clock in the shop do you like best?
Point to a digital clock that says 3:01.
How did people tell time before clocks were invented?

4

The sun is up

The earth is a gigantic spinning ball. When the side of the earth we live on faces the sun, the sun lights up the earth. We have daylight. On the other side of the earth, it is dark. People are sleeping.

Early in the morning, the sun begins to rise out of the east. This time of day is called *dawn*. The darkness brightens as the sun begins to face this side of the earth. The air is still cool from the night as the sun peeks over the horizon.

The people who live and work on this city corner are beginning their day. Let's watch them! Anna is taking her dog, Chester, for a walk. She is holding a morning newspaper under her arm. She says good morning to the man sweeping the steps of the movie theater.

The baker comes to work very early so that people can buy fresh bread for breakfast. The fruit and vegetable shop is just opening. How can you tell?

Mr. Kinney waves to his wife and daughter, Brigitte. He is on his way to work. Philip is kissing his mother good-bye before he leaves for school. His friends are waiting for him. One friend is looking at his watch. What time do you think it is?

Picture talk

Are the street lights on or off? Why?
Which of the things in the picture do you do in the morning?

Time for lunch

On sunny days, the sky is always brightest around noon. In the summer, the sun is high over our heads. Our shadows are short, and the sun is hot. But the earth never stands still. As the earth turns, the sun gets lower in the western sky. Noon has passed. This time of day is called afternoon.

At the beginning of the afternoon, schools and businesses have a break. It's lunchtime! The restaurant on this city corner is crowded. People enjoy looking out at the street while they eat.

A wonderful smell of baking is coming from the Costas' apartment. Mary is starving. She can't wait to sink her teeth into a sandwich and a piece of freshly-baked chocolate cake. Philip's father is coming home for lunch. What is he carrying?

Much has happened in the world since the early morning. Look at the newspaper stand. Are there any newspapers left? Soon the delivery truck will arrive with bundles of the afternoon edition. The window in the bakery is nearly empty. Everyone wants the baker's fresh bread, rolls, and cakes for lunch! Point to people who have bought some of her bread.

Picture talk
How is the movie billboard changing?
Are there fewer or more people on the sidewalks in the afternoon than in the morning? Why?
Tell a story about any two people in this picture.

Good evening

Look! The sun has just set in the west. There is still a little light, but not for long. This time of the day is called *dusk* or *twilight*. As the earth keeps turning away from the sun, the sky becomes darker. The air is cooler. Stars twinkle in the sky. Now it is evening.

Most of the shops are closed. The storekeepers are sweeping up. The baker's assistant has locked the bakery door. He is taking home the last loaf of bread. Is it still fresh?

Delicious aromas drift through the air. Dinners are cooking in many homes. The restaurant is crowded again. Some friends are meeting in the park. Several people are lining up for a movie. Can you see someone whose friend is late?

Mr. Kinney is home from work. He has been playing with little Brigitte, and now he is putting her to bed. She is very tired. Little children need plenty of sleep.

Evening can be a time for homework, hobbies, games, or chores. Some people enjoy watching television. For many people, evening is a time just to relax.

Picture talk
Point to some people who are working.
What time do you eat dinner?
Mr. and Mrs. Neto are having a quiet time. He is reading the newspaper and she is knitting.
What do you do when you have a quiet evening at home?

11

Nighttime

The sun has completely disappeared. It is now lighting up the other side of the world. The sky on our side is dark. It's nighttime. Many people are asleep. We rest at the darkest time and wake up when it grows light again.

Mr. Neto is turning on his television set. He likes to stay up late and watch scary movies! His wife has already gone to bed. Philip is fast asleep, but his mother is still up reading a book.

Brigitte has woken up. She sometimes gets thirsty during the night. She is having a drink with her parents. Mary was reading in bed. She fell asleep with her light on. Will her mother check on Mary before she goes to bed?

Mary's mother, Mrs. Costa, is looking out into the street. The street is almost empty. The restaurant is closing up for the night. The movie is over. The last people are just leaving. Mrs. Costa sees a tired grey cat. She closes the curtains. "It's time to go to bed!" she yawns. "But first I'll check on Mary."

Picture talk

Why are so many apartment curtains closed?
What is visiting the rooftop garden?
When will the sun return to this city corner?
When the sun is directly opposite us at night, the sky is darkest. This time is called *midnight*.
Tell a spooky story about midnight.

My favorite day

A day is a morning, afternoon, evening, and night. There are seven days in a week. The weekdays, when most people go to work or school, are called Monday, Tuesday, Wednesday, Thursday, and Friday. The other two days are called Saturday and Sunday. They are also known as the weekend.

Loni's favorite day

Hi! I'm Loni. My favorite day of the week is Saturday. On Saturdays I go to the stable for my riding lessons. I love riding horses. I am not very good though. I fall off a lot!

There are about four weeks in a month. Every fourth Saturday, my riding stable has a horse show. People come from nearby towns to compete. They bring their horses in trailers.

Some horses compete in the driving competitions. They pull carriages around the markers. I think the most exciting competition is jumping. Sometimes the horses knock down the jumps and sometimes they don't. You never know what will happen!

I am always disappointed when the horse show is over. I count the days until the next one.

Picture talk

Find two photographers and three judges.
What is being sold in the tents?
Find the rider who has fallen off a horse.
When will the next horse show be?
What is your favorite day of the week? Why?

Summertime

Summer comes to the northern hemisphere at the end of June and lasts until the end of September. In the southern hemisphere, the sun is warmest in the months of December, January, February, and March.

In the summer, the sun brings more hours of sunlight and warmer weather. The trees on the Pearson farm are full of leaves. Flowers are in full bloom. The corn and wheat are growing in the fields. The blackberries on the bushes are almost ripe.

There are insects in the air. Can you see the butterflies that have come out of their cocoons? All the animals have plenty of food to eat because the summer grass is long. The female deer or doe has a baby or fawn. The fawn is nursing from its mother. The robin's nest holds two blue eggs and two tiny birds! How many baby squirrels can you count?

School is closed for the summer. The whole Pearson family is outside. They like the warm summer weather. Joy is throwing bread crumbs to the ducks and ducklings. Dale is riding his bicycle. Mr. Pearson is relaxing while Ron splashes in the wading pool. Summer is a time for fun in the sun!

Picture talk

Is this a hot day? How can you tell?
How do you feel when you go to bed and it is still light outside?
Summer is a good time for vacations. Can you see a family going on vacation?

19

The falling leaves

In the northern hemisphere, autumn begins in late September and lasts through October, November, and part of December. In the southern hemisphere, the autumn months are March, April, May, and June.

The part of the earth that we live on is tilted away from the sun in autumn. The air cools, and there are fewer hours of daylight. The leaves die and fall off the trees. That is why autumn is also known as *fall*. The colors of the dying leaves are beautiful. Only evergreen trees remain green through autumn and winter.

The Pearsons are gathering the ripe apples. Perhaps they will use them to make applesauce or apple crisp! Joy and Dale are picking the ripe blackberries. How can you tell that Dale likes blackberries? The vegetables in the garden are ready to be eaten. The corn and wheat in the fields have been gathered or *harvested*.

Some birds do not like the cool weather. The robins have flown or *migrated* to the south where it is warm. They will find food there. The squirrels are storing nuts, and most of the animals are growing long hair. Why?

Picture talk

Mr. Pearson is at the front of the house. How is he preparing for winter?

Name the autumn activities taking place in the picture.

What are the autumn activities you enjoy most?

What do you smell or hear in the autumn?

It's cold outside

Winter comes to the northern half of the world in late December and lasts until the end of March. In the southern half of the world, the winter months are June, July, August, and September.

Do you like wintertime? Some people travel south to get away from the cold. But many people like to ski, toboggan, and skate. Some people drive snowmobiles. Children build snowmen and snow forts.

The Pearsons are busy, but the groundhogs and bears are sleeping. They *hibernate* all winter long because there is no food for them to eat during the winter months. Some animals stay awake all winter. Their food supply is small and they must work hard to survive. The squirrels eat the nuts that they have stored away during the autumn. The deer scratch in the snow. They are looking for food.

Many birds have migrated to warmer places where food is plentiful. But not all birds migrate. Do you see the woodpecker in the tree? He is pecking to find insects that live in the bark. The Pearsons put out food for the birds that do not migrate. Can you see the bird feeder? Joy and Dale like to watch the birds from the window.

Picture talk
How do the Pearsons dress to keep warm?
What has Joy just seen?
Where are the horses and cows?
What is wintertime like where you live?

Time drags, time flies!

"Grace, I'll see you after the race," said Alan. "Good luck!"

Grace smiled nervously. She was thinking of all the things she had to do before she rode in the motocross competition. Would she have time for everything? The morning seemed so short! She sprang into action. She took a test run on her bike, filled the tires, and registered for the race. She then hurried to change into her racing suit.

Alan, on the other hand, had nothing to do all morning. He was not in the race. He offered to help Grace get ready, but Grace liked to do everything herself. That way she knew it was done properly. Alan wandered around the grounds for what seemed like ages. Time seemed to pass very slowly. Would the race *never* start?

Finally the racers assembled at the starting line. They were off! Then, almost before he knew it, Alan saw the racers approaching the finish. Was Grace in the lead? Yes! Alan couldn't wait to congratulate his friend, but he was disappointed that the race had finished so quickly!

Picture talk
Which biker do you think will come second?
Why did the time go so quickly for Grace?
When did time go slowly for Alan?
When does time seem to pass quickly for you?

Past, present, and future

Can you imagine a time when there were no radios, television sets, or airplanes? Only one hundred years ago, none of these things had been invented. When your great-grandparents were children, they could not sit down after school to watch television. They could not hear the newest songs on the radio or travel through the skies on airplanes.

Now these things are part of our present. Even things that your parents did not have when they were children, such as video cassette recorders, are common today. In 1969, American astronauts landed on the moon. Since then, many people have gone into space. As time passes, space travel may be as common as traveling in a plane.

What do you think the future will bring? Will people travel to different planets for vacations? Do you think you will ever travel on a spaceship? Which planet would you visit? We know that we must always live in our own time, the present, but we can remember the past, and we can always dream about the future!

Picture talk
Write or talk about something that has happened to you in the past.
Draw a picture of the clothes of the future.

Ways to talk about time

Time is so much a part of our lives that we have many words to use when we talk about it. Many of these words are in the story that follows. There are over 50 of them. Some of the words are repeated. Count each one separately, including the ones in the headings. Also count the things that measure time, such as clocks. Can you find all the time words?

Another day for Carol

"Carol, wake up. It's time to get out of bed." Carol heard her mother's voice. She looked at her clock. It was only seven. Carol rolled over slowly and tried to get back to her dream. It had been a wonderful dream about the future. Funny little cars flew through the air. She was just about to fly off in one when her mother's voice woke her.

"Carol, time to get up." The voice was getting louder. A few minutes before, her mother had called her from thc kitchen. Now she was calling from the stairs. Soon she would be in Carol's room.

Carol quickly jumped out of bed. "Coming!" she called. "I'll be down in a minute."

Carol got dressed. Then she tied up her shoes. After Carol brushed her hair, she did up the buttons on her sweater. She noticed that the sleeves were too short now. Carol remembered her grandfather measuring her height last year. He had marked it on the measuring board with a red pen. It was time for Carol to be measured again. She had grown. She was taller now!

Time for breakfast

Carol ran downstairs. Just as she sat down at the breakfast table, her father stood up. "Good morning, Carol," her father said. He looked at his watch. "I have to leave now or I'll be late for work." He waved good-bye and dashed out the door.

Carol asked her brother, Rick, to pass the cereal. "Cereal again?" Rick asked. "You had cereal for breakfast the day before yesterday. You had it yesterday, too. Now you want cereal again today.

You will probably want it tomorrow and the day after that. It's time for you to eat something different for breakfast.''

Carol smiled at her older brother. He was always grumpy in the morning. In the afternoon, he would begin to smile. In the evening, he would begin to laugh. By the time night came, he would be telling jokes.

A daydream

As Carol ate her breakfast, she looked out the window at the falling snow. Winter was Carol's favorite season. It was a time to bundle up in warm clothes. It was a time for making snowmen and drinking hot chocolate. Carol thought about autumn. This past autumn had been fun. She had enjoyed raking the leaves that fell from the trees. Carol's thoughts drifted to the coming spring when all the snow would melt and the birds would return. Then summer would be here. Summer seemed a long way in the future.

Back to the present!

"Carol, it's time for school. It's eight o'clock."

Carol was brought back to the present with a jump. Her time for remembering the past and looking forward to the future was over.

She finished her cereal in ten seconds flat and ran to get ready for school. In a few minutes, she was waiting for the school bus. In an hour she would be at school. Carol sighed. What a busy day it had already been. And the day had just begun!

Time zones

Do you know what time it is? You may know what time it is here, but the time is different in other parts of the world.

Time is different around the world because the sun brings day and night to different places at different times. In 1884, people decided to find a system so they could know what time it was in other places. They called this system *standard time*. The world was divided into 24 time sections. Each section was called a *zone*. Whenever we are in one zone, the time is always the same. It is *standard*. But as soon as we travel outside the zone, the time changes.

How do we know the time in each zone? One special zone was chosen as the place where time was set. It was the zone in which Greenwich, England is located. Imagine it is 1:00 pm in the Greenwich zone. In the zone to the east of Greenwich, the time is one hour later, or 2:00 pm. Two zones east of Greenwich, the time is two hours later, or 3:00 pm. One zone west of Greenwich, the time is one hour earlier, or 12 noon.

This may seem like a crazy way to measure time, but the world needs to change times in different zones. We have to set our clocks according to the sun as it rises and sets. When the sun is the highest, the time must say noon where you live. And at the same time, on the other side of the world where it is night, the clocks have to read midnight!

Travel with the Cooks

Mr. and Mrs. Cook are traveling from their home in Seattle, Washington, to New Delhi, India. Can you help them adjust their watches as they travel? Don't forget! If they travel west, they subtract one hour for every time zone they pass through. If they travel east, they add one hour for every time zone they pass through. You may need to use your atlas!

1. The Cooks stopped over in Toronto, Canada to visit relatives. When they landed in Toronto, Mr. Cook's sister, Betty, said, "Oh, good. It's 5 o'clock. You're just in time for dinner!" The Cooks shook their heads. "No," they said. "We've just had lunch. We must have crossed 3 time zones to get here!" What time do their watches say?

2. The next week, the Cooks flew from Toronto to Amsterdam, the Netherlands. They left at 7:00 pm. When they landed, they realized that they had crossed 6 more time zones. The clocks in Amsterdam said 8:00 am, but the Cooks did not want breakfast! What time did their watches say? How long did their flight take?

3. After spending a few days in Amsterdam, the Cooks hopped on their connecting flight to New Delhi, India. When they arrived, they realized their watches, which had been reset in Amsterdam, had to be reset again! Their watches said 1:00 am, but they had crossed 4 time zones, and India also adds a half-hour to standard time. What time is it when the Cooks arrive in New Delhi?

4. The Cooks yawned. They wanted to be in bed, but the morning in New Delhi had just begun! The bus from the airport took them to this bus terminal downtown. Can you figure out how long the ride took them by looking at this picture?

Answers:

1. 2:00 pm; 2. 2:00 am, 7 hours; 3. 5:30 am; 4. 45 minutes

Time dictionary

calf The young of the cow.

day The time of light between dawn and sunset. A day is also a period of twenty-four hours from one midnight to the next. The earth makes one full turn on its axis in one day.

digital Having digits, which are any of the numerals from 0 through 9, so named from counting on the fingers or digits.

doe A female deer.

equator The imaginary line that goes around the middle of the earth exactly halfway between the North Pole and the South Pole.

evergreen A tree, shrub, or plant with leaves or needles that stay green all through the year.

fawn A young deer.

foal A young horse.

future The time that is to come.

harvest To gather and bring in a crop when the crop is ripe.

hemisphere One half of the earth's surface. The earth is divided by the equator into the Northern and Southern Hemispheres. It can also be divided into the Eastern and Western Hemispheres.

hibernate To spend the winter asleep or in an inactive state. Many animals, such as bears, groundhogs, and snakes, hibernate.

hour A unit of time that equals sixty minutes. Twenty-four hours make one day and one night.

hour hand The hand, usually short, on a clock or watch which points to the hour.

migrate To move from one place or climate to another at the change of the season. Birds migrate in autumn and spring.

minute A unit of time that equals sixty seconds. Sixty minutes equals one hour.

minute hand The hand, usually long, on a clock or watch which points to the minutes that pass.

month One of the twelve parts into which the year is divided.

past Time that has gone by.

present The time existing or going on now. Not past or future.

ripe Fully grown. Ready to be used as food.

season One of the four parts of the year. The seasons are determined by the position of the earth in its orbit around the earth. The four seasons are spring, summer, autumn, and winter.

second A unit of time that is one of the sixty parts of a minute. Sixty seconds equal one minute.

standard Anything that is widely used or usual.

standard time The official time of any place. It is based on the distance of a region from Greenwich, England. The earth is divided into twenty-four time zones.

week A period of seven days, usually beginning on a Sunday and counted through to the next Saturday.

weekend Saturday and Sunday.

year The period of time during which the earth makes one complete circle around the sun. A year is 365 days long. A year is made up of 12 months.

3456789   BP   Printed in Canada   43210987